AF268654

Pickles packed into a jar.
Pickles wondering where they are.

Release the pickles
and you will see,
pickles are just like
you and me!

Pickles come in all colours, shapes and sizes.

Pickles are fun,
and full of surprises!

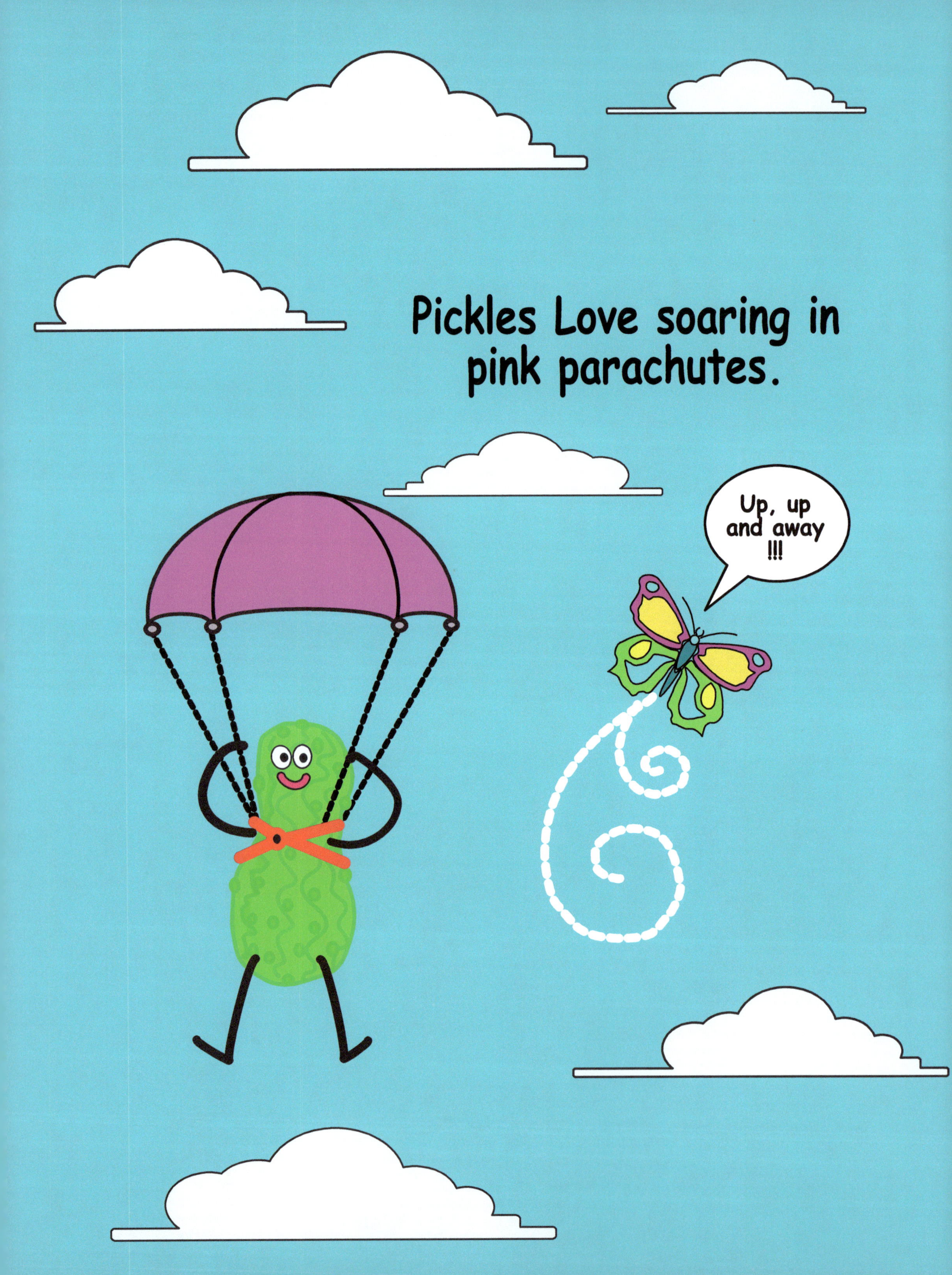

Pickles Love soaring in pink parachutes.

Pickles Love horsies
and bright cowboy boots.

Pickles Love singing
and playing guitars.

Pickles Love driving
in cool little cars.

Pickles Love pizza, pickles Love ham.
PIZZA!
PINEAPPLE!
What a ham !!!

Pickles Love Grandmother's strawberry jam!

Pickles Love trying on
big silly hats!

Pickles Love paintings of
funny orange cats!

Pickles on pancakes with syrup sounds awful.

Pickles with ice cream,
and on a waffle.

Pickles Love going on
big mountain hikes.

Pickles Love
riding on
cool yellow
bikes.

Pickles Love magic
and
performing great tricks.

Pickles Love
Kung-Fu
and
high-flying kicks.
Everbody was
Kung Fu
fighting
HA
HA

Pickles Love helping
by doing the dishes.

Pickles Love diving and scaring the fishes!

Pickles Love gardens,
and watering flowers.

Pickles Love drumming for hours and hours.

Pickles Love counting and saving their money.

CHOCOLATE MILK
Well that's just GROSS
Pickles in chocolate milk isn't funny.

Pickles play sports
until they are sweaty.

Pasta

Pickles Love great big bowls of spaghetti.

Pickles on rollerskates
scooting along.

Pickles on trampolines singing a song.
Row,row,row your boat, gently down the stream
Merrily, merrily merrily, merrily
Life is but a dream!
boing boing boing

Pickles play bagpipes from evening till dawn.

ACH!
GET
TEE BED
!!!

Pickles Love helping by mowing the lawn.

Pickles Love dancing
for the whole world to see!

Pickles are
AWESOME
just like
you and me !

Big Gratitude

To my family for all the Love,
and for always
making me laugh!

For my blessings,
(that I dont count often enough)

To the
Big Guy Upstairs,
Thanks for EVERYTHING!!!

LOVE THE WORLD,
Heather New

About the Author
Heather New

I am an artist living in Canada,
and my biggest joy comes from
my family and friends.
I Love music and art,but most of all,
I Love being silly and laughing!

I spent years volunteering as a clown,
and especially loved
painting the faces of children
from all cultures, races
and backgrounds.

I have attained worldwide attention
for engraving motorcycles,and now
I have decided to try something new
by writing a children's book.

It is my hope that we will all look
for common ground
with those we perceive to be
different from ourselves.

Wouldn't it be a great world
if we could figure out a way to be friends
with everyone ?

P.S.
Look for the 4-leaf clovers! They are everywhere!
You only need to discover them....